CUPCAKES & COOKIES

 LAKELAND

Lakeland and ACP Magazines Ltd hereby exclude all liability to the extent permitted by law for any errors or omission in this book and for any loss, damage or expense (whether direct or indirect) suffered by a third party relying on any information contained in this book.

This book was created in 2010 for Lakeland by AWW Books, an imprint of Octopus Publishing Group Ltd, based on materials licensed to it by ACP Magazines Ltd, a division of PBL Media Pty Limited.

54 Park St, Sydney
GPO Box 4088, Sydney, NSW 2001
phone (02) 9282 8618; fax (02) 9267 9438
acpbooks@acpmagazines.com.au;
www.acpbooks.com.au

OCTOPUS PUBLISHING GROUP
Design – Chris Bell
Food Director - Pamela Clark

Published for Lakeland in the United Kingdom by Octopus Publishing Group Limited

Endeavour House
189 Shaftesbury Avenue
London WC2H 8JY
United Kingdom
phone + 44 (0) 207 632 5400;
fax + 44 (0) 207 632 5405
aww@octopusbooks.co.uk;
www.octopusbooks.co.uk
www.australian-womens-weekly.com

Printed and bound in China

A catalogue record for this book is available from the British Library.

ISBN 978-1-907428-13-5

The Department of Health advises that eggs should not be consumed raw. This book contains some dishes made with raw or lightly cooked eggs. It is prudent for vulnerable people such as pregnant and nursing mothers, invalids, the elderly, babies and young children to avoid uncooked or lightly cooked dishes made with eggs. Once prepared, these dishes should be kept refrigerated and used promptly.

This book also includes dishes made with nuts and nut derivatives. It is advisable for those with known allergic reactions to nuts and nut derivatives and those who may be potentially vulnerable to these allergies, such as pregnant and nursing mothers, invalids, the elderly, babies and children to avoid dishes made with nuts and nut oils. It is also prudent to check the labels of pre-prepared ingredients for the possible inclusion of nut derivatives.

Some of the recipes in this book have appeared in other publications.

CUPCAKES & COOKIES

Indulge in the taste of 'home sweet home' with this scrumptious selection of cupcake and cookie recipes. So simple to make, you'll love these 53 sweet bakes for everyday and special occasions – melt-in-the mouth cookies and biscuits, tempting home-made cupcakes and teatime treats, from madeleines to biscotti.

One of an exciting new series of cookbooks from Lakeland, *Cupcakes & Cookies* is packed with delicious colour photos and expert hints, tips and techniques for beginners and experienced cooks alike.

With every recipe triple-tested® for perfect results, these excellent cookbooks are sure to be some of the best-loved on your kitchen bookshelf. To discover the rest of the range, together with our unrivalled selection of creative kitchenware, visit one of our friendly Lakeland stores or shop online at www.lakeland.co.uk.

CONTENTS

HINTS & TIPS

COOKIES & BISCUITS

Biscuits have existed almost as long as man has known how to grind grain to make flour. Most of the breads of ancient history probably resembled the hard, flat cakes we now know as biscuits.

The word 'biscuit' dates from Roman times. Their armies marched on *panis biscoctus* – *panis* meaning 'bread', *bis* meaning 'twice' and *coctus* meaning 'cooked'. The word travelled to France where it was translated as biscuit, Italy as biscotti and Spain as biscochitos.

Maintaining the military tradition, ship's biscuits and hard tack travelled the world as a hard, nutritionally filling foodstuff that kept well when stored in relatively airtight containers such as tins. In the United States, biscuits are more likely to be called crackers or cookies. When Americans use the term biscuit, they are usually referring to scones.

America has also given the world the biscuit known as the tollhouse or chocolate chip cookie, perhaps invented, but certainly popularised by Ruth Wakefield who introduced it on the menu of her Whitman, Massachusetts Tollhouse restaurant in the 1930s.

As the recipes in this book illustrate, cookie variations are only limited by the imagination. We're sure you'll find some to stimulate yours in this collection of quick and easy tea-time treats.

Oven trays

It's important to use the correct trays to ensure even baking and browning. We use flat aluminium trays, which have little or no sides. This allows the heat to circulate properly and ensures even browning. Grease the trays lightly with cooking-oil spray or a light and even brushing with a pastry brush that has been dipped in melted butter.

You can bake two or more trays of cookies at once, so long as the trays don't touch the sides of the oven or the door when it is closed. There should be at least 2cm of space around each tray to allow for heat circulation. To cook the biscuits evenly, you'll need to swap the trays around halfway through baking. Some ovens have hot spots, and if this is the case with yours, it's a good idea to rotate the trays as well, to help with even browning.

Preparation and mixing

Have all ingredients out on the worktop at room temperature before you start. Take care not to over-beat the butter and sugar mixture; beat the butter until it's smooth then add the sugar and beat just until the ingredients are combined. Over-beating can give a too-soft mixture which can cause the biscuits to spread excessively. Add the sifted dry ingredients in two batches to make mixing easier. You may need to transfer the butter and sugar mixture to a larger bowl to make stirring in the dry ingredients easier.

Piping bags

Some of our recipes use a piping bag to force the mixture into decorative shapes. There is also a device known as a biscuit or cookie pusher which you can use, though the thickness of the biscuits will vary from ours and you'll need to adjust the baking times. You can also make a basic piping bag by snipping a small hole in the corner of a sturdy, clean plastic bag, though, without fancy tubes, you will only be able to pipe tubular and round shapes.

Testing if cooked

Cookies generally feel soft in the oven and become firmer as they cool. If they are very soft, loosen with a palette knife or spatula and lift on to a wire rack to cool.

Some of the crisper varieties are cooled on the oven trays; follow each recipe's instructions.

A good test for most types of biscuit is to push the biscuit on the tray gently with your finger; if it moves without breaking, the biscuit is cooked.

Storage

Store biscuits and cookies in an airtight container. They must be completely cold before storing or they will soften. Biscuits which are to be filled with jam, cream or icing are best filled on the day of serving. If unfilled un-iced biscuits soften, they can be re-crisped by placing them on oven trays and heating in a moderate oven for about 5 minutes.

Freezing

To freeze un-iced or unfilled biscuits, place the cooked cooled biscuits in an airtight container, with sheets of baking parchment between the layers.

Trouble shooting

• If the cookies spread on the tray, the mixture could be too soft due to over-beating the butter and sugar, or the ingredients were measured incorrectly, the wrong flour (such as self-raising when the recipe calls for plain flour) was used or the oven was not hot enough.

• If the cookies are too hard, the ingredients may have been measured incorrectly, the biscuits baked too long or at too high a temperature or the wrong type of oven trays used.

• If the cookies are too soft, they may not have been baked long enough, or they may have been stacked on top of each other during cooling. Most cookies need air circulating around them to crisp. They generally need to rest on the trays for a few minutes to harden slightly before transferring to wire racks to cool completely.

• If the cookies are too brown underneath, the trays may have been overgreased; excess greasing attracts heat to the base of the cookie. Incorrect oven position and temperature could also be to blame. Excess sweetening (sugar, honey etc) will also cause overbrowning.

CUPCAKES

It's not so long ago when cupcakes or fairy cakes were considered children's party fare, quick to whip up and easy to pass around in convenient individual servings. If they were to grace the afternoon tea table they might be dressed up with a bit of icing or as butterfly cakes, with a scoop of cake from the centre cut in half to make wings and a dollop of jam and cream added to make them worthy of adult attention.

In recent years however, cupcakes have grown up and become sophisticated stars of the cake kingdom. The reasons for their popularity remain the same – they're portable, easy to serve and there will be no concerns about under-catering if you make one for every guest plus a few spares.

What has changed is the way they are decorated and presented – clever cooks now know that what is basically a simple cake can be turned into a mini masterpiece with a few easy trimmings and presentation on a decorative plate. The French, of course, have known this for centuries – many of the elegant little confections known as petits fours are simply miniature cakes decorated with flair.

The term cupcake is probably a reference to the original recipe for the cake mixture – a cupful of butter, a cupful of flour, sugar… much as a pound cake used a pound of each of the core ingredients. Or it's possible that the name also refers to the small containers in which they were baked – most teacups are fired at much higher temperatures than a domestic oven can ever achieve, so are quite safe as baking dishes. Either way, there are references to individual cakes in English cookbooks from the 18th century. Light fruit cakes known as queen cakes were also popular and baked in fluted or heart-shaped moulds.

These days, just about any cake mixture can be used to make the new-age cupcake. The butter cake recipe remains popular, but so too are chocolate and mud cake mixtures, flourless orange and almond cakes, gingerbread, fresh fruit and poppyseed recipes. Icings and decorations are limited only by your imagination and we're sure that the selection presented in this book will inspire a whole new generation of variations and adaptations.

Baking tips

Each recipe specifies the baking time for the cake size we used, but there is no reason why you can't make the cakes in different sizes as long as you adjust the baking times. You can buy paper cases to fit most individual cake pans. Measured across the base a large muffin case is 6.5cm, freeform 6cm, standard muffin 5cm, mini muffin 3cm and foil cases 2.5cm. Paper cases are available from supermarkets, cookware shops, chefs' supply shops and cake decorating suppliers.

If you don't have enough muffin pans, or your oven is not big enough to cook them all at once, don't worry, it's fine to cook in batches and stand the remaining mixture for the relatively short cooking times.

Decorative touches

Sugared fruits and flowers, chocolate decorations, coloured sprinkles, cachous, hundreds and thousands and the entire sweet shop of confectionery options can quickly elevate the simple cupcake to a work of art.

Coloured sugar, jelly crystals and desiccated coconut also provide a simple, but effective contrast to the icing on a cupcake. Place a small quantity of caster or granulated sugar (depending on the texture you prefer) or coconut in a plastic bag, add a tiny amount of food colouring and work the colouring through by massaging the plastic bag between your fingers. As with all food colourings, start with a tiny drop of colour and add more if you need a deeper colour. Coloured sugar will keep in a jar at room temperature indefinitely.

Colourings

Many varieties of food colourings are available from supermarkets, cake decorating suppliers and craft shops. They come in liquid, gel, powder and paste forms and should all be used in minute quantities first to determine strength.

Concentrated pastes are more expensive than regular liquid colours, but they last longer, blend easily and are suitable for both pastel and strong colours. Coloured icing can become lighter or darker on standing, so if you plan to ice the cake a day in advance, test the colour-fastness of the colouring you plan to use by tinting a small quantity of icing beforehand.

Lustre, or edible colour, is a powder available from cake decorating shops and craft shops in metallic shades. You apply it with a paintbrush. Edible glitter is a non-metallic decoration for cakes.

Decorating tools and techniques

The recipe for basic butter cream is included in Mallow Moments on page 73 but you can also use cream cheese frosting,

ready-made soft icing (fondant), marzipan, whipped cream or a host of other frostings and icings.

A piping bag may be useful for decorating cupcakes. Other useful pieces of equipment include metal or plastic icing tubes that allow you to better control the flow of the icing as you pipe writing on the cake and non-stick rolling pins for rolling soft icing.

Useful accessories to look out for in the supermarket include candy cake decorations, assorted lettering and shapes such as flowers, hearts and stars and tubes of coloured piping gel which can be used to write or draw outlines on cakes.

Presentation

For special occasions, such as weddings and birthdays, it's become popular to make a table centrepiece of cupcakes. A tiered cake stand is ideal for this, and you can decorate the spaces between the cakes with ribbon bows or fresh flowers. If you don't have a tiered cake stand, improvise by stacking three or four individual stands of varying sizes on top of each other.

EVERYDAY COOKIES

GOLDEN PECAN TWISTS

2 tablespoons golden syrup
40g finely chopped pecans
125g butter, softened
¼ teaspoon vanilla extract
75g caster sugar
1 egg yolk
150g plain flour

1 Preheat oven to 180°C/160°C fan-assisted. Grease oven trays; line with baking parchment.
2 Combine half of the golden syrup with nuts in small bowl.
3 Beat butter, extract, sugar, remaining golden syrup and egg yolk in small bowl with electric mixer until light and fluffy. Stir in sifted flour.
4 Shape rounded teaspoons of mixture into balls; roll each ball into 12cm log. Twist each log into a loop, overlapping one end over the other. Place twists on trays 3cm apart; top each twist with ½ teaspoon nut mixture. Bake about 10 minutes; cool twists on trays.

prep + cook time 35 minutes
makes 30

CRUNCHY MUESLI COOKIES

90g rolled oats
150g plain flour
220g caster sugar
2 teaspoons ground cinnamon
35g dried cranberries
55g finely chopped dried apricots
70g slivered almonds
125g butter
2 tablespoons golden syrup
½ teaspoon bicarbonate of soda
1 tablespoon boiling water

1 Preheat oven to 150°C/130°C fan-assisted. Grease oven trays; line with baking parchment.
2 Combine oats, flour, sugar, cinnamon, dried fruit and nuts in large bowl.
3 Melt butter with golden syrup in small saucepan over low heat; add combined soda and the boiling water. Stir warm butter mixture into dry ingredients.
4 Roll level tablespoons of mixture into balls, place on trays 5cm apart; flatten with hand. Bake about 20 minutes; cool cookies on trays.

prep + cook time 40 minutes
makes 36

OAT & BRAN BISCUITS

150g plain flour
60g unprocessed bran
60g rolled oats
½ teaspoon bicarbonate of soda
60g butter, chopped
110g caster sugar
1 egg
2 tablespoons water,
   approximately

1 Process flour, bran, oats, soda and butter until crumbly; add sugar, egg and enough of the water to make a firm dough. Knead dough on lightly floured surface until smooth; cover, refrigerate 30 minutes.
2 Preheat oven to 180°C/160°C fan-assisted. Grease oven trays; line with baking parchment.
3 Divide dough in half; roll each half between sheets of baking parchment to about 5mm thickness. Cut dough into 7cm rounds; place on trays 2cm apart. Bake about 15 minutes. Stand biscuits on trays 5 minutes; transfer to wire rack to cool.

prep + cook time 30 minutes (+ refrigeration)
makes 30

BROWN SUGAR & GINGER SNAPS

200g brown sugar
3 teaspoons ground ginger
2 tablespoons finely chopped
   stem ginger
300g plain flour
200g butter, chopped
1 egg

1 Preheat oven to 160°C/140°C fan-assisted.
2 Process sugar, ground and stem gingers, flour and butter until mixture resembles breadcrumbs. Add egg; process until mixture forms a ball.
3 Turn dough onto lightly floured surface, knead gently until smooth. Roll rounded teaspoons of mixture into balls, place about 5cm apart on lightly greased oven trays; flatten slightly with a floured fork.
4 Bake about 25 minutes or until browned; stand biscuits on trays for 5 minutes, before lifting onto wire racks to cool.

prep + cook time 40 minutes
makes 60

CHOCOLATE WHEATIES

90g butter
100g firmly packed brown sugar
1 egg, beaten lightly
20g desiccated coconut
25g wheatgerm
120g wholemeal plain flour
75g self-raising flour
150g dark eating chocolate,
   melted

1 Preheat oven to 180°C/160°C fan-assisted.

2 Beat butter and sugar in small bowl with electric mixer until smooth; add egg, beat until combined.

3 Stir in coconut, wheatgerm and flours. Roll rounded teaspoons of mixture into balls, place about 3cm apart on lightly greased oven trays; flatten with a fork.

4 Bake about 12 minutes or until lightly browned. Cool on trays.

5 Dip half of each biscuit in melted chocolate; leave to set on wire racks.

prep + cook time 40 minutes
makes 35

MAPLE-SYRUP BUTTER COOKIES

125g butter, softened
½ teaspoon vanilla extract
80ml maple syrup
110g plain flour
35g cornflour

1 Preheat oven to 180°C/160°C fan-assisted. Grease oven trays; line with baking parchment.
2 Beat butter, extract and maple syrup in small bowl with electric mixer until light and fluffy; stir in combined sifted flours. Spoon mixture into piping bag fitted with 1cm fluted tube.
3 Pipe stars about 3cm apart onto trays. Bake about 15 minutes; cool cookies on trays.

prep + cook time 35 minutes
makes 24

DATE & WALNUT SCROLLS

125g butter, softened
75g caster sugar
1 teaspoon ground cardamom
1 egg
225g plain flour
100g walnuts, roasted, ground
    finely
280g dried dates, chopped
    coarsely
55g caster sugar, extra
2 teaspoons finely grated
    lemon rind
80ml lemon juice
¼ teaspoon ground cardamom,
    extra
125ml water

1 Beat butter, sugar, cardamom and egg in small bowl with electric mixer until combined. Stir in sifted flour and walnuts.
2 Knead dough on floured surface until smooth; divide into two portions. Roll each portion between sheets of baking parchment to 15cm x 30cm rectangles; refrigerate 20 minutes.
3 Meanwhile, stir dates, extra sugar, rind, juice, extra cardamom and the water in medium saucepan over heat, without boiling, until sugar is dissolved; bring to a boil. Reduce heat, simmer, uncovered, stirring occasionally, about 5 minutes or until mixture is thick and pulpy. Transfer to large bowl; refrigerate 10 minutes.
4 Spread filling evenly over the two rectangles, leaving 1cm border. Using paper as a guide, roll rectangles tightly from short side to enclose filling. Wrap rolls in baking parchment; refrigerate 30 minutes.
5 Preheat oven to 190°C/170°C fan-assisted. Grease oven trays; line with baking parchment.

6 Trim edges of roll; cut each roll into 1cm slices. Place slices cut-side up on oven trays; bake about 20 minutes.

prep + cook time 1 hour
(+ refrigeration)
makes 28

WHOLEMEAL ROSEMARY BUTTER ROUNDS

125g butter, softened
2 teaspoons finely grated orange
    rind
220g brown sugar
200g wholemeal self-raising flour
100g walnuts, roasted, chopped
    coarsely
100g raisins, halved
2 teaspoons dried rosemary
80ml orange juice
50g desiccated coconut
60g rolled oats

1 Preheat oven to 180°C/160°C
fan-assisted. Grease oven trays;
line with baking parchment.
2 Beat butter, rind and sugar in
small bowl with electric mixer until
combined. Transfer to medium
bowl; stir in flour then remaining
ingredients.
3 Roll rounded tablespoons of
mixture into balls, place about
5cm apart on oven trays; flatten
slightly. Bake about 15 minutes.
Cool on trays.

prep + cook time 35 minutes
makes 28

PEANUT BUTTER COOKIES

125g butter, softened
70g crunchy peanut butter
165g brown sugar
1 egg
225g plain flour
½ teaspoon bicarbonate of soda
70g roasted unsalted peanuts,
    chopped coarsely

1 Preheat oven to 180°C/160°C fan-assisted. Grease oven trays; line with baking parchment.
2 Beat butter, peanut butter, sugar and egg in small bowl with electric mixer until smooth; do not over-mix. Transfer mixture to medium bowl; stir in sifted flour and soda, then nuts.
3 Roll level tablespoons of mixture into balls; place 5cm apart on trays, flatten with floured fork. Bake about 12 minutes; cool on trays.

prep + cook time 25 minutes
makes 30

VANILLA KISSES

125g butter, softened
110g caster sugar
1 egg
50g plain flour
35g self-raising flour
100g cornflour
30g custard powder
vienna cream
60g butter, softened
½ teaspoon vanilla extract
120g icing sugar
2 teaspoons milk

1 Preheat oven to 200°C/180°C fan-assisted. Grease oven trays; line with baking parchment.
2 Beat butter, sugar and egg in small bowl with electric mixer until light and fluffy. Stir in sifted dry ingredients, in two batches.
3 Spoon mixture into piping bag fitted with 1cm fluted tube. Pipe 3cm rosettes about 3cm apart on trays. Bake about 10 minutes; cool on trays.
4 Meanwhile, make vienna cream. Sandwich biscuits with vienna cream.
vienna cream Beat butter and extract in small bowl with electric mixer until as white as possible; gradually beat in sifted icing sugar and milk, in two batches.

prep + cook time 25 minutes
makes 20

SPECIAL
OCCASION
COOKIES

HONEY JUMBLES

60g butter
110g brown sugar
270g golden syrup
1 egg, beaten lightly
375g plain flour
75g self-raising flour
½ teaspoon bicarbonate of soda
1 teaspoon ground cinnamon
½ teaspoon ground cloves
2 teaspoons ground ginger
1 teaspoon mixed spice
icing
1 egg white
240g icing sugar
2 teaspoons plain flour
1 tablespoon lemon juice,
   approximately
pink food colouring

1 Preheat oven to 160°C/140°C fan-assisted. Grease oven trays.
2 Stir butter, sugar and syrup in medium saucepan over low heat until sugar dissolves. Cool 10 minutes.
3 Transfer mixture to large bowl; stir in egg and sifted dry ingredients, in two batches. Knead dough on floured surface until it loses its stickiness. Cover; refrigerate 30 minutes.
4 Divide dough into eight portions. Roll each portion into a 2cm-thick sausage; cut each sausage into five 6cm lengths. Place about 3cm apart on oven trays; round ends with lightly floured fingers, flatten slightly.
5 Bake about 15 minutes; cool on trays.
6 Meanwhile, make icing. Spread jumbles with pink and white icing.
icing Beat egg white lightly in small bowl; gradually stir in sifted icing sugar and flour, then enough juice to make icing spreadable. Place half the mixture in another small bowl; tint with colouring. Keep icings covered with a damp tea towel while in use.

prep + cook time 40 minutes (+ refrigeration)
makes 40

MONTE CARLO BISCUITS

180g butter, softened
1 teaspoon vanilla extract
110g brown sugar
1 egg
185g self-raising flour
105g plain flour
¼ teaspoon bicarbonate of soda
50g desiccated coconut
110g raspberry jam
vienna cream
60g butter, softened
½ teaspoon vanilla extract
120g icing sugar
2 teaspoons milk

1 Preheat oven to 200°C/180°C fan-assisted. Grease oven trays; line with baking parchment.
2 Beat butter, extract and sugar in small bowl with electric mixer until just combined; beat in egg. Stir in sifted flours, soda and coconut in two batches.
3 Roll 2 level teaspoons of mixture into ovals; place on trays about 5cm apart. Flatten slightly; use back of fork to roughen surface. Bake about 7 minutes.
4 Meanwhile, make vienna cream.
5 Lift biscuits onto wire rack to cool. Sandwich biscuits with vienna cream and jam.
vienna cream Beat butter and extract in small bowl with electric mixer until as white as possible; gradually beat in sifted icing sugar and milk, in two batches.

prep + cook time 40 minutes
makes 28

ALMOND & PLUM CRESCENTS

225g plain flour
60g ground almonds
55g caster sugar
2 teaspoons finely grated lemon
  rind
90g cream cheese, softened
90g butter, chopped
2 tablespoons buttermilk
1 egg white
20g flaked almonds, crushed
  lightly
filling
60g finely chopped pitted prunes
80g plum jam
55g caster sugar
½ teaspoon ground cinnamon

1 Process flour, ground almonds, sugar and rind until combined. Add cream cheese and butter, pulse until crumbly. Add buttermilk, process until ingredients come together.
2 Knead dough on floured surface until smooth. Divide dough in half. Roll each half between sheets of baking parchment until large enough to be cut into 22cm rounds; cut dough using 22cm cake tin as a guide. Discard excess dough. Cover rounds; refrigerate 30 minutes.
3 Preheat oven to 180°C/160°C fan-assisted. Grease oven trays; line with baking parchment.
4 Make filling by combining ingredients in small bowl.
5 Cut each round into eight wedges, spread each wedge with a little filling mixture; roll from the wide end into a crescent shape. Place on oven trays, brush with egg white, sprinkle with flaked almonds. Bake about 25 minutes. Cool on trays.

prep + cook time 55 minutes (+ refrigeration)
makes 16

HOT CROSS BUN COOKIES

125g butter, softened
150g caster sugar
1 egg
40g finely chopped mixed peel
80g currants
300g self-raising flour
1 teaspoon mixed spice
2 teaspoons milk
2 tablespoons ground almonds
100g marzipan
2 tablespoons apricot jam,
  warmed, strained

1 Preheat oven to 160°C/140°C fan-assisted. Grease oven trays, line with baking parchment.
2 Beat butter, sugar and egg in small bowl with electric mixer until light and fluffy. Stir in peel, currants, sifted flour and spice, and milk in two batches.
3 Roll rounded teaspoons of mixture into balls; place about 5cm apart on oven trays.
4 Knead ground almonds into marzipan. Roll marzipan into 5mm diameter sausages; cut into 4cm lengths.
5 Brush cookies with a little milk; place marzipan crosses on cookies, press down gently.
6 Bake about 15 minutes. Brush cookies with jam; cool on trays.

prep + cook time 40 minutes
makes 48

DOUBLE CHOC-CHIP CHILLI COOKIES

250g butter, softened
1 teaspoon vanilla extract
165g caster sugar
165g brown sugar
1 egg
300g plain flour
25g cocoa powder
1 teaspoon bicarbonate of soda
400g dark eating chocolate,
    chopped coarsely
candied chillies
55g caster sugar
60ml water
3 fresh red chillies, chopped finely

1 Preheat oven to 180°C/160°C fan-assisted. Grease oven trays; line with baking parchment.
2 Make candied chillies.
3 Beat butter, extract, sugars and egg in small bowl with electric mixer until light and fluffy; transfer to large bowl.
4 Stir in sifted flour, cocoa and soda in two batches. Stir in chilli and chocolate.
5 Roll level tablespoons of dough into balls; place about 5cm apart on oven trays. Bake about 12 minutes. Cool on trays.
candied chillies Stir sugar and the water in small saucepan over heat until sugar dissolves. Add chilli, boil, 2 minutes; cool. Strain, discard syrup.

prep + cook time 45 minutes
makes 48

MUD CAKE SANDWICHES

250g butter, softened
330g brown sugar
2 eggs
450g plain flour
75g self-raising flour
50g cocoa powder
2 tablespoons cocoa powder, extra

chocolate mud cake
150g butter, chopped
100g dark eating chocolate, chopped coarsely
220g caster sugar
125ml water
2 tablespoons coffee liqueur
150g plain flour
2 tablespoons cocoa powder
2 egg yolks

chocolate ganache
80ml pouring cream
200g dark eating chocolate, chopped coarsely

1 Preheat oven to 170°C/150°C fan-assisted. Grease two 20cm x 30cm baking tins; line with a strip of baking parchment, extending paper 2cm above edges of tins.
2 Make chocolate mud cake.
3 Make chocolate ganache.
4 Beat butter, sugar and eggs in small bowl with electric mixer until combined. Transfer mixture to large bowl; stir in sifted flours and cocoa, in two batches. Knead dough on floured surface until smooth; divide in half, roll each portion between sheets of baking parchment until 5mm thick. Cover; refrigerate 30 minutes.
5 Preheat oven to 180°C/160°C fan-assisted. Grease oven trays; line with baking parchment.
6 Using 6.5cm round cutter, cut 48 rounds from dough. Place about 3cm apart on oven trays. Bake about 12 minutes. Cool on wire racks.
7 Spread ganache onto underside of cookies; sandwich a mud cake round between two cookies.
8 Using a paper heart template, dust cookies with extra cocoa.

chocolate mud cake Combine butter, chocolate, sugar, the water and liqueur in small saucepan. Stir over low heat until smooth. Place mixture in medium bowl; cool 10 minutes. Whisk in sifted flour and cocoa, then egg yolks. Divide mixture among tins. Bake about 25 minutes. Cool cakes in tins. Using 6.5cm round cutter, cut 12 rounds from each cake.

chocolate ganache Bring cream to a boil in small saucepan; remove from heat. When bubbles subside, add chocolate; stir until smooth. Refrigerate until spreadable.

prep + cook time 1 hour 15 minutes (+ refrigeration)
makes 24

JAFFA JELLY CAKES

110g caster sugar

2 eggs

150g plain flour

2 tablespoons caster sugar, extra

400g dark eating chocolate, melted

3 slices glacé orange, cut into wedges

orange jelly

250ml orange juice

2 tablespoons orange marmalade

85g packet orange jelly crystals

1 Make orange jelly.

2 Preheat oven to 180°C/160°C fan-assisted. Grease oven trays; line with baking parchment.

3 Spread sugar evenly over base of shallow oven tray; heat in oven until sugar feels hot to touch. Beat eggs in small bowl with electric mixer on high speed for 1 minute; add hot sugar, beat about 10 minutes or until mixture is thick and will hold its shape.

4 Meanwhile, sift flour three times. Fit large piping bag with plain 1cm tube.

5 Transfer egg mixture to large bowl, fold in sifted flour. Place mixture into piping bag. Pipe 4cm rounds of mixture onto oven trays, about 3cm apart.

6 Sprinkle each round evenly with extra sugar. Bake each tray, one at a time, about 4 minutes. Cool on trays.

7 Lift jelly from tin to board. Using a 4cm round cutter, cut out 25 shapes.

8 Top each sponge with a round of jelly, place on wire rack over tray; coat with chocolate. When chocolate is almost set, top with glacé orange wedges.

orange jelly Combine juice and marmalade in small saucepan, bring to a boil; remove from heat. Add jelly crystals, stir until dissolved; cool. Line a deep 23cm square cake tin with baking parchment, extending paper 5cm above edges of tin. Pour jelly into tin; refrigerate until set.

prep + cook time 1 hour 10 minutes (+ refrigeration and standing)
makes 25

CHOC-MALLOW WHEELS

125g butter, softened
165g brown sugar
1 egg
225g plain flour
35g self-raising flour
25g cocoa powder
28 marshmallows
80g raspberry jam
375g dark eating chocolate,
    chopped
1 tablespoon vegetable oil

1 Beat butter, sugar and egg in small bowl with electric mixer until combined. Stir in sifted flours and cocoa, in two batches.

2 Knead dough on floured surface until smooth. Roll between sheets of baking parchment until 3mm thick. Cover; refrigerate 30 minutes.

3 Preheat oven to 180°C/160°C fan-assisted. Grease oven trays; line with baking parchment.

4 Using 7cm round fluted cutter, cut 28 rounds from dough. Place about 3cm apart on trays.

5 Bake about 12 minutes. Cool on wire racks.

6 Turn half the biscuits base-side up; place on oven tray. Use scissors to cut marshmallows in half horizontally. Press four marshmallow halves, cut-side down, onto biscuit bases on tray. Bake 2 minutes.

7 Melt chocolate in medium heatproof bowl over medium saucepan of simmering water. Remove from heat; stir in oil.

8 Spread jam over bases of remaining cookies; press onto softened marshmallow. Stand 20 minutes or until marshmallow is firm. Dip wheels into chocolate; smooth away excess chocolate using metal spatula. Place on baking parchment-lined trays to set.

prep + cook time 55 minutes
(+ refrigeration and standing)
makes 14

COFFEE WALNUT CREAMS

250g plain flour
125g cold butter, chopped
55g caster sugar
½ teaspoon vanilla extract
1 egg, beaten lightly
18 walnut halves
walnut butter cream
185g unsalted butter, softened
120g icing sugar
1 tablespoon cocoa powder
1 tablespoon instant coffee
    granules
125g walnuts, chopped finely
coffee icing
160g icing sugar
2 teaspoons instant coffee
    granules
1 tablespoon hot water
1 teaspoon butter

1 Sift flour into medium bowl, rub in butter. Stir in sugar, extract and egg.
2 Knead dough on floured surface until smooth. Divide in half. Roll, in half between sheets of baking parchment until 3mm thick. Refrigerate 30 minutes.
3 Preheat oven to 180°C/160°C fan-assisted. Grease oven trays; line with baking parchment.
4 Using 5.5cm round cutter, cut out 36 rounds. Place on oven trays; bake about 12 minutes. Cool on wire racks.
5 Meanwhile, make walnut butter cream.
6 Sandwich cookies with butter cream; refrigerate 30 minutes.
7 Meanwhile, make coffee icing.
8 Spread cookies with icing and top with walnut halves.

walnut butter cream Beat butter and sifted icing sugar in small bowl with electric mixer until light and fluffy. Beat in combined cocoa, coffee and the water. Stir in nuts.

coffee icing Sift icing sugar into small heatproof bowl, stir in combined coffee and the water; add butter. Stir over small saucepan of simmering water until icing is spreadable.

prep + cook time 55 minutes (+ refrigeration)
makes 18

PASSIONFRUIT CREAM BISCUITS

125g butter, softened
2 teaspoons finely grated lemon
  rind
75g caster sugar
2 tablespoons golden syrup
150g self-raising flour
100g plain flour
60ml passionfruit pulp
passionfruit cream
2 tablespoons passionfruit pulp
90g butter, softened
160g icing sugar

1 Beat butter, rind and sugar in small bowl with electric mixer until light and fluffy. Add golden syrup, beat until combined. Stir in sifted dry ingredients and passionfruit pulp.
2 Turn dough onto floured surface, knead gently until smooth. Cut dough in half; roll each portion between sheets of baking parchment to 5mm thickness. Refrigerate 30 minutes.
3 Preheat oven to 160°C/140°C fan-assisted. Grease oven trays; line with baking parchment.
4 Cut 25 x 4cm fluted rounds from each portion of dough; place about 2.5cm apart on trays.
5 Bake biscuits about 10 minutes. Cool on trays.
6 Meanwhile, make passionfruit cream.
7 Spoon passionfruit cream into piping bag fitted with 5mm fluted nozzle. Pipe cream onto half the biscuits; top with remaining biscuits. Serve dusted with a little extra sifted icing sugar, if you like.

passionfruit cream Strain passionfruit pulp through fine sieve into small jug, discard seeds. Beat butter and sugar in small bowl with electric mixer until light and fluffy. Beat in passionfruit juice.

prep + cook time 45 minutes (+ refrigeration)
makes 25
tip You need about 6 passionfruit for this recipe.

PISTACHIO ALMOND CRISPS

3 egg whites
110g caster sugar
pinch ground cardamom
150g plain flour
80g blanched almonds
70g roasted unsalted pistachios

1 Preheat oven to 160°C/140°C fan-assisted. Grease 30cm-square piece of foil.

2 Beat egg whites in small bowl with electric mixer until soft peaks form. Gradually add sugar, beating until dissolved between additions. Transfer mixture to medium bowl; fold in sifted dry ingredients and nuts.

3 Spoon mixture onto foil, shape into 7cm x 25cm log. Enclose firmly in foil; place on oven tray.

4 Bake log about 45 minutes or until firm. Turn log out of foil onto wire rack to cool.

5 Reduce oven to 120°C/100°C fan-assisted.

6 Using serrated knife, slice log thinly. Place slices close together in single layer on oven trays. Bake about 20 minutes or until crisp; transfer to wire racks to cool.

prep + cook time 1 hour 30 minutes
makes 65
tip If you have an electric knife you can cut the slices really finely.

CUPCAKES

LEMON CURD CREAMS

90g butter, softened
1 teaspoon finely grated lemon
   rind
110g caster sugar
2 eggs
150g self-raising flour
2 tablespoons milk
decorations
250ml whipping cream
160g lemon curd
2 tablespoons icing sugar

1 Preheat oven to 180°C/160°C fan-assisted. Line eight holes of 12-hole (80ml) muffin pan with paper cases.

2 Beat butter, rind, sugar, eggs, sifted flour and milk in small bowl with electric mixer on low speed until ingredients are combined. Increase speed to medium; beat until mixture has changed to a paler colour. Drop 3 tablespoons of mixture into paper cases.

3 Bake about 20 minutes. Stand cakes in pan 5 minutes before turning, top-side up, onto wire rack to cool.

4 Beat cream in small bowl with electric mixer until firm peaks form.

5 Cut a deep triangular hole into the top of cold cakes; reserve lids. Spoon whipped cream into large piping bag fitted with a large fluted tube. Fill holes with lemon curd. Pipe cream over curd, drizzle with a little extra curd. Position lids in centre of each cake. Dust cakes with a little sifted icing sugar.

prep + cook time 45 minutes
makes 8

SPOTTY GINGER BUTTERMILK CAKES

110g light brown sugar
75g plain flour
75g self-raising flour
¼ teaspoon bicarbonate of soda
1 teaspoon ground ginger
½ teaspoon ground cinnamon
¼ teaspoon ground nutmeg
90g butter, softened
1 egg
60ml buttermilk
2 tablespoons golden syrup
decorations
250g ready-made white icing
yellow food colouring
110g apricot jam, warmed,
  strained

1 Preheat oven to 170°C/150°C fan-assisted. Line nine holes of 12-hole (80ml) muffin pan with paper cases.
2 Sift dry ingredients into small bowl, add remaining ingredients; beat mixture with electric mixer on low speed until combined. Increase speed to medium; beat until mixture has changed to a paler colour.
3 Drop 3 tablespoons of mixture into paper cases. Bake about 35 minutes. Stand cakes in pan 5 minutes before turning, top-side up, onto wire rack to cool.
4 Divide ready-made white icing in half. Tint one portion yellow, leave remaining portion white. Roll each colour, one at a time, between sheets of baking parchment until 5mm thick. Using 2cm cutter, cut rounds, quite close together, from both pieces of icing. Place white rounds in the holes left in the yellow icing, and the yellow rounds in the holes left in the white icing. Re-roll both pieces of icing between sheets of baking parchment to ensure the rounds are in place.

5 Brush cold cakes with a little jam. Using 8cm cutter, cut rounds from each piece of icing; position rounds on cakes.

prep + cook time 1 hour
makes 9

CHOC MINT CRUSH CAKES

60g dark eating chocolate,
   chopped coarsely
160ml water
90g butter, softened
220g light brown sugar
2 eggs
100g self-raising flour
2 tablespoons cocoa powder
40g ground almonds
dark chocolate ganache
125ml pouring cream
200g dark eating chocolate,
   chopped coarsely
decorations
24 mint boiled sweets

1 Preheat oven to 170°C/150°C fan-assisted. Line 12-hole (80ml) muffin pan with paper cases.
2 Stir chocolate and the water in small saucepan over low heat until smooth.
3 Beat butter, sugar and eggs in small bowl with electric mixer until light and fluffy. Stir in sifted flour and cocoa, ground almonds and warm chocolate mixture. Drop 3 tablespoons of mixture into paper cases.
4 Bake about 25 minutes. Stand cakes in pan 5 minutes before turning, top-side up, onto wire rack to cool.
5 Make dark chocolate ganache.
6 Place mint sweets in a small plastic resealable bag. Using rolling pin, gently tap sweets to crush slightly. Spread cold cakes with chocolate ganache; top with crushed mint sweets.

dark chocolate ganache Bring cream to the boil in small saucepan; remove from heat. When bubbles subside, add chocolate; stir until smooth. Cool 15 minutes.

prep + cook time 50 minutes
makes 12

CHOCOLATE PEANUT HEAVEN CAKES

60g dark eating chocolate,
   chopped coarsely
160ml water
90g butter, softened
220g light brown sugar
2 eggs
100g self-raising flour
2 tablespoons cocoa powder
40g ground almonds
**whipped milk choc peanut
   ganache**
250ml pouring cream
410g milk eating chocolate,
   chopped coarsely
280g crunchy peanut butter
decorations
250g peanut brittle, crushed

1 Preheat oven to 170°C/150°C
fan-assisted. Line 12-hole (80ml)
muffin pan with paper cases.
2 Stir chocolate and the water in
small saucepan over low heat until
smooth.
3 Beat butter, sugar and eggs in
small bowl with electric mixer until
light and fluffy. Stir in sifted flour
and cocoa, ground almonds and
warm chocolate mixture. Drop
3 tablespoons of mixture into
paper cases.
4 Bake about 25 minutes. Stand
cakes in pan 5 minutes before
turning, top-side up, onto wire
rack to cool.
5 Make whipped milk choc
peanut ganache. Spoon ganache
into large piping bag fitted with a
large fluted tube. Pipe generous
swirls of ganache on cold cakes;
sprinkle with crushed peanut
brittle.

**whipped milk choc peanut
ganache** Bring cream to the boil
in small saucepan; remove from
heat. When bubbles subside,
add chocolate; stir until smooth.
Transfer mixture to small bowl.
Cover; refrigerate 30 minutes. Beat
with an electric mixer until light
and fluffy. Marble peanut butter
through ganache.

prep + cook time 50 minutes
(+ refrigeration)
makes 12

LITTLE CHOCOLATE & COCONUT SPONGES

4 eggs
165g caster sugar
100g self-raising flour
35g cocoa powder
90g butter, melted
1 tablespoon hot water
160ml whipping cream
2 tablespoons caster sugar, extra
15g flaked coconut
dark chocolate ganache
200g dark eating chocolate,
    chopped coarsely
160ml pouring cream

1 Preheat oven to 180°C/160°C fan-assisted. Grease two 9-hole large (125ml) muffin pans.
2 Beat eggs in small bowl with electric mixer until thick and creamy. Gradually add sugar, a tablespoon at a time, beating until sugar is dissolved between additions. Transfer mixture to large bowl; fold in sifted flour, cocoa, then butter and hot water. Spoon mixture into pans.
3 Bake cakes 12 minutes; turn out immediately onto wire racks to cool.
4 Meanwhile, make chocolate ganache.
5 Beat cream and extra sugar in small bowl with electric mixer until soft peaks form. Split cooled sponges in half. Spread bases with cream; replace tops. Spread ganache over cakes, sprinkle with coconut.

dark chocolate ganache Bring cream to a boil in small saucepan; remove from heat. When bubbles subside, add chocolate; stir until smooth. Remove from heat; stand until thickened.

prep + cook time 50 minutes
makes 18

CHECKERBOARD CARROT CAKES

250ml vegetable oil
300g firmly packed light brown
  sugar
3 eggs
720g coarsely grated carrot
110g coarsely chopped walnuts
375g self-raising flour
½ teaspoon bicarbonate of soda
2 teaspoons mixed spice
butter cream
125g butter, softened
240g icing sugar
2 tablespoons milk
white food colouring
decorations
liquorice allsorts

1 Preheat oven to 180°C/160°C fan-assisted. Line 18 holes of two 12-hole (80ml) muffin pans with paper cases.
2 Beat oil, sugar and eggs in small bowl with electric mixer until thick. Transfer mixture to large bowl; stir in carrot, nuts, then sifted dry ingredients. Drop 3 tablespoons of mixture into paper cases.
3 Bake about 30 minutes. Stand cakes in pans 5 minutes before turning, top-side up, onto wire racks to cool.
4 Make butter cream. Spread cold cakes with butter cream.
5 Remove orange fondant sections from liquorice allsorts; cut each section into four squares. Make a checkerboard pattern on the cakes with the fondant squares.

butter cream Beat butter in small bowl with electric mixer until as white as possible; beat in sifted icing sugar and milk, in two batches. Tint butter cream white with food colouring.

prep + cook time 55 minutes
makes 18
tip To save waste you could use the different coloured fondant sections from the liquorice allsorts and decorate each cake with a different colour.

MARBLED CHOCOLATE CAKES

dark chocolate mud cake
90g butter, chopped coarsely
75g dark eating chocolate,
   chopped coarsely
150g caster sugar
125ml milk
75g plain flour
35g self-raising flour
1 tablespoon cocoa powder
1 egg
white chocolate mud cake
90g butter, chopped coarsely
75g white eating chocolate,
   chopped coarsely
110g caster sugar
80ml milk
100g plain flour
35g self-raising flour
1 egg
dark chocolate ganache
80ml pouring cream
200g dark eating chocolate,
   chopped coarsely
white chocolate ganache
2 tablespoons pouring cream
100g white eating chocolate,
   chopped coarsely

1 Preheat oven to 160°C/140°C fan-assisted. Grease two six-hole large (180ml) muffin pans.
2 Make dark mud cake by combining butter, chocolate, sugar and milk in medium saucepan; stir over low heat until smooth. Transfer to medium bowl; cool 10 minutes. Whisk in sifted flours and cocoa, then whisk in egg.
3 Make white chocolate mud cake by combining butter, chocolate, sugar and milk in medium saucepan; stir over low heat until smooth. Transfer to medium bowl; cool 10 minutes. Whisk in sifted flours, then whisk in egg.
4 Drop alternate spoonfuls of mixtures into pan holes. Pull skewer back and forth through cake mixture several times for a marbled effect. Bake about 30 minutes.
5 Meanwhile, make dark and white chocolate ganache.
6 Stand cakes in pans 5 minutes before turning, top-side up, onto wire racks to cool.

7 Spread cold cakes with dark chocolate ganache; dollop cakes with spoonfuls of white chocolate ganache. Using knife, swirl back and forth through ganache for marbled effect.
dark chocolate ganache Stir cream and chocolate in small saucepan over low heat until smooth. Cool 15 minutes.
white chocolate ganache Bring cream to a boil in small saucepan; remove from heat. When bubbles subside, add chocolate; stir until smooth. Cool 15 minutes.

prep + cook time 1 hour 10 minutes
makes 12

MALLOW MOMENTS

90g butter, softened
1 teaspoon vanilla extract
110g caster sugar
2 eggs
150g self-raising flour
2 tablespoons milk
butter cream
125g butter, softened
240g icing sugar
2 tablespoons milk
decorations
280g toasted coconut-covered
   marshmallows

1 Preheat oven to 180°C/160°C fan-assisted. Line eight holes of 12-hole (80ml) muffin pan with paper cases.
2 Beat butter, extract, sugar, eggs, sifted flour and milk in small bowl with electric mixer on low speed until ingredients are combined. Increase speed to medium; beat until mixture has changed to a paler colour. Drop 3 tablespoons of mixture into paper cases.
3 Bake about 20 minutes. Stand cakes in pan 5 minutes before turning, top-side up, onto wire rack to cool.
4 Make butter cream.
5 Use scissors to cut marshmallows into small pieces. Spread cold cakes thickly with butter cream; top with marshmallow pieces.

butter cream Beat butter in small bowl with electric mixer until as white as possible; beat in sifted icing sugar and milk, in two batches.

prep + cook time 45 minutes
makes 8

tip If you can't find coconut-covered marshmallows use traditional marshmallows or mini marshmallows instead.

FAIRY CAKES WITH GLACÉ ICING

125g butter, softened
1 teaspoon vanilla extract
150g caster sugar
3 eggs
225g self-raising flour
60ml milk
glacé icing
240g icing sugar
1 teaspoon butter
2 tablespoons milk,
    approximately

1 Preheat oven to 180°C/160°C fan-assisted. Line two deep 12-hole patty pans with paper cases.
2 Beat butter, extract, sugar, eggs, flour and milk in medium bowl with electric mixer at low speed until just combined. Increase speed to medium; beat about 3 minutes or until mixture is smooth and paler in colour. Drop slightly rounded tablespoons of mixture into paper cases.
3 Bake cakes about 20 minutes. Turn, top-side up, onto wire racks to cool.
4 Meanwhile, make glacé icing; top cakes with icing.
glacé icing Sift icing sugar into small heatproof bowl; stir in butter and enough milk to give a firm paste. Set bowl over small saucepan of simmering water; stir until icing is spreadable.

prep + cook time 40 minutes
makes 24

COCONUT ICE CAKES

60g butter, softened
½ teaspoon coconut essence
110g caster sugar
1 egg
20g desiccated coconut
110g self-raising flour
120g soured cream
2 tablespoons milk
coconut ice icing
160g icing sugar
50g desiccated coconut
1 egg white, beaten lightly
pink food colouring

1 Preheat oven to 160°C/140°C fan-assisted. Line 18 holes of two 12-hole (40ml) deep flat-based muffin pans with paper cases.
2 Beat butter, essence, sugar and egg in small bowl with electric mixer until light and fluffy. Stir in the coconut, sifted flour, soured cream and milk, in two batches. Divide mixture into paper cases.
3 Bake cakes about 20 minutes. Stand cakes 5 minutes before turning top-side up onto wire rack to cool.
4 Meanwhile, make coconut ice icing.
5 Drop alternate rounded teaspoons of white and pink icing onto cakes; marble over the top of each cake.
coconut ice icing Sift icing sugar into medium bowl; stir in coconut and egg white. Place half the mixture in small bowl; tint with pink food colouring.

prep + cook time 1 hour
makes 18
tip Coconut essence is available from specialist cake shops and on line.

MINI CHOCOLATE HAZELNUT CAKES

100g dark eating chocolate, chopped coarsely
180ml water
100g butter, softened
220g brown sugar
3 eggs
25g cocoa powder
110g self-raising flour
35g ground hazelnuts
whipped hazelnut ganache
80ml whipping cream
180g milk eating chocolate, chopped finely
2 tablespoons hazelnut-flavoured liqueur

1 Preheat oven to 180°C/160°C fan-assisted. Grease 12-hole large (125ml) muffin pan.
2 Make whipped hazelnut ganache.
3 Meanwhile, combine chocolate and the water in medium saucepan; stir over low heat until smooth.
4 Beat butter and sugar in small bowl with electric mixer until light and fluffy. Add eggs, one at a time, beating until just combined between additions (mixture might separate at this stage, but will come together later); transfer mixture to medium bowl. Stir in warm chocolate mixture, sifted cocoa and flour, and ground hazelnuts.
5 Divide mixture among pans; bake about 20 minutes. Stand cakes 5 minutes; turn, top-sides up, onto wire rack to cool. Spread ganache over cakes.

whipped hazelnut ganache Bring cream to a boil in small saucepan; remove from heat. When bubbles subside, add chocolate; stir until smooth. Stir in liqueur; transfer mixture to small bowl. Cover; stand about 2 hours or until just firm. Beat ganache in small bowl with electric mixer until mixture changes to a pale brown colour.

prep + cook time 1 hour (+ standing)
makes 12

GLUTEN-FREE BERRY CUPCAKES

125g butter, softened
2 teaspoons finely grated lemon
  rind
165g caster sugar
4 eggs
240g ground almonds
40g desiccated coconut
100g rice flour
1 teaspoon bicarbonate of soda
150g frozen mixed berries
1 tablespoon desiccated coconut,
  extra

1 Preheat oven to 180°C/160°C fan-assisted. Grease 12-hole (80ml) muffin pan.
2 Beat butter, rind and sugar in small bowl with electric mixer until light and fluffy. Add eggs, one at a time, beating until just combined between additions (mixture will separate at this stage, but will come together later); transfer to large bowl. Stir in ground almonds, coconut, sifted flour and soda, then the berries.
3 Divide mixture among muffin pan holes; bake about 25 minutes. Stand cupcakes 5 minutes; turn, top-sides up, onto wire rack to cool. Sprinkle with extra coconut.

prep + cook time 45 minutes
makes 12

MINI CARROT CAKES

80ml vegetable oil
110g light brown sugar
1 egg
240g coarsely grated carrot
40g finely chopped walnuts
110g self-raising flour
½ teaspoon mixed spice
1 tablespoon pumpkin seeds,
   chopped finely
1 tablespoon finely chopped
   dried apricots
1 tablespoon finely chopped
   walnuts, extra
lemon cream cheese icing
90g cream cheese, softened
30g unsalted butter, softened
1 teaspoon finely grated lemon
   rind
240g icing sugar

1 Preheat oven to 160°C/140°C fan-assisted. Line 18 holes of two 12-hole (40ml) deep flat-based muffin pans with paper cases.
2 Beat oil, sugar and egg in small bowl with electric mixer until thick and creamy. Stir in carrot and walnuts, then sifted flour and spice. Divide mixture into paper cases.
3 Bake cakes about 20 minutes. Stand cakes 5 minutes before turning top-side up onto wire rack to cool.
4 Meanwhile, make lemon cream cheese icing.
5 Spoon lemon cream cheese icing into piping bag fitted with 2cm fluted nozzle; pipe icing onto cakes. Sprinkle cakes with combined pumpkin seeds, apricots and extra walnuts.

lemon cream cheese icing Beat cream cheese, butter and rind in small bowl with electric mixer until light and fluffy; gradually beat in sifted icing sugar.

prep + cook time 45 minutes
makes 18

ORANGE SUGARED ALMOND CAKES

90g butter, softened
2 teaspoons finely grated orange
 rind
110g caster sugar
2 eggs
150g self-raising flour
2 tablespoons milk
orange glacé icing
320g icing sugar
1 teaspoon softened butter
2 tablespoons strained orange
 juice, approximately
decorations
8 blue sugared almonds

1 Preheat oven to 180°C/160°C fan-assisted. Line eight holes of 12-hole (80ml) muffin pan with paper cases.

2 Beat butter, rind, sugar, eggs, sifted flour and milk in small bowl with electric mixer on low speed until ingredients are combined. Increase speed to medium; beat until mixture has changed to a paler colour. Drop 3 tablespoons of mixture into paper cases.

3 Bake about 20 minutes. Stand cakes in pan 5 minutes before turning, top-side up, onto wire rack to cool.

4 Make orange glacé icing. Working with one cold cake at a time, spread top with icing. Position a sugared almond in the centre of each cake before icing has set.

orange glacé icing Sift icing sugar into small heatproof bowl; stir in butter and enough of the juice to make a thick paste. Stir over small saucepan of simmering water until icing is spreadable.

prep + cook time 45 minutes
makes 8
tip We used blue sugared almond, available from specialist cake and wedding shops and websites, but you can use any colour.

HUMMINGBIRD CAKES WITH COCONUT CRUST

440g canned crushed pineapple
   in syrup
150g plain flour
75g self-raising flour
½ teaspoon bicarbonate of soda
½ teaspoon ground cinnamon
½ teaspoon ground ginger
220g light brown sugar
40g desiccated coconut
220g mashed over-ripe banana
2 eggs, beaten lightly
180ml vegetable oil
coconut crust
225g shredded coconut
110g light brown sugar
3 eggs, beaten lightly

1 Preheat oven to 180°C/160°C
fan-assisted. Line 18 holes of two
12-hole (80ml) muffin pans with
paper cases.
2 Drain pineapple over medium
bowl, pressing with spoon to
extract as much syrup as possible.
Reserve 60ml of the syrup.
3 Sift flours, soda, spices and
sugar into large bowl. Stir in
drained pineapple, reserved
syrup, coconut, banana, egg and
oil. Divide mixture among paper
cases. Bake 10 minutes.
4 Meanwhile, make coconut crust.
Spoon crust over cakes; return to
oven, bake about 15 minutes.
5 Stand cakes in pans 5 minutes
before turning, top-side up, onto
wire racks to cool. Lightly dust
with sifted icing sugar to serve,
if you like.
coconut crust Combine
ingredients in medium bowl.

prep + cook time 50 minutes
makes 18
tip You need two large (460g)
over-ripe bananas to get the
required amount of mashed
banana.

ORANGE BLOSSOM CAKES

125g butter, softened
2 teaspoons finely grated orange
  rind
150g caster sugar
2 eggs
150g self-raising flour
50g plain flour
40g ground almonds
65g dried cranberries
60ml orange juice
2 tablespoons milk
modelling fondant
2 teaspoons gelatine
1½ tablespoons water
2 teaspoons glucose syrup
240g icing sugar
80g icing sugar, extra
green, yellow, orange and pink
  food colouring
butter cream
90g butter, softened
¼ teaspoon orange essence
160g icing sugar
1 tablespoon milk
green, yellow, orange and pink
  food colouring

1 Make modelling fondant;
reserve a walnut-sized portion.
2 Dust surface with icing sugar,
roll remaining fondant to a
thickness of approximately 3mm.
Cut out 18 flowers using 3cm
cutter or 36 flowers using 2cm
cutter.
3 Divide reserved fondant into
four; knead one of the colourings
into each portion. Roll tiny balls
for flower centres; lightly brush
flower centres with water to secure
coloured balls.
4 Preheat oven to 180°C/160°C
fan-assisted. Line 6-hole large or
12-hole standard muffin pan with
paper cases.
5 Beat butter, rind, sugar and
eggs in small bowl with electric
mixer until light and fluffy.
6 Stir in sifted flours, ground
almonds, cranberries, juice and
milk. Divide mixture among cases;
smooth surface.
7 Bake large cakes about
35 minutes, small cakes about
25 minutes. Turn cakes onto wire
rack to cool.

8 Make butter cream.
9 Spread cakes with butter cream;
decorate with flowers.
modelling fondant Sprinkle
gelatine over the water in cup;
stand cup in small saucepan of
simmering water, stirring until
gelatine is dissolved, add glucose.
Place half the sifted icing sugar in
small bowl, stir in gelatine mixture.
Gradually stir in remaining sifted
icing sugar, knead on surface
dusted with extra sifted icing
sugar until smooth. Enclose in
cling film.
butter cream Beat butter and
essence in small bowl with electric
mixer until light and fluffy. Beat in
sifted icing sugar and milk, in two
batches. Beat in a little of desired
colouring.

prep + cook time 1 hour
30 minutes for larger cakes
makes 6 large or 12 standard size
cupcakes

WHITE CHOCOLATE CUPCAKES

250g butter, chopped
150g white eating chocolate, chopped coarsely
440g caster sugar
250ml milk
225g plain flour
75g self-raising flour
1 teaspoon vanilla extract
2 eggs, beaten lightly
fluffy icing
220g caster sugar
80ml water
2 egg whites
decorations
small flowers
silver cachous

1 Preheat oven to 160°C/140°C fan-assisted. Line two 12-hole (80ml) muffin pans with paper cases.

2 Combine butter, chocolate, sugar and milk in medium saucepan; stir over low heat, without boiling, until smooth. Transfer mixture to medium bowl; cool 15 minutes.

3 Whisk sifted flours, then extract and egg into chocolate mixture. Divide mixture among cases; bake about 35 minutes. Turn cakes, top-side up, onto wire rack to cool.

4 Make fluffy icing.

5 Spread cakes with fluffy icing; decorate with flowers and cachous.

fluffy icing Combine sugar and the water in small saucepan; stir over low heat, without boiling, until sugar dissolves. Bring to a boil; boil, uncovered, without stirring, about 3 minutes or until syrup is slightly thick. Remove syrup from heat, allow bubbles to subside. Test the syrup by dropping 1 teaspoon of it into cold water. The syrup should form a ball of soft sticky toffee when rolled between fingertips (114°C on a sugar thermometer). The syrup should not colour; if it does, discard it. Just before syrup reaches the correct temperature, beat egg whites in a small bowl with electric mixer until firm. When syrup is ready, allow bubbles to subside then, with electric mixer operating on medium speed, pour a thin stream of syrup onto egg whites. If syrup is added too quickly to the egg whites, icing will not thicken. Continue to beat on high speed about 5 minutes or until thick. Icing should be barely warm by now.

prep + cook time 1 hour 40 minutes
makes 24 cakes
tip For a soft icing of marshmallow consistency, ice cakes on the day of serving as the following day the icing will lose its gloss. Add flowers a few hours ahead, or very delicate flowers as close to serving as possible.

BANANA BLUEBERRY CUPCAKES

125g butter
125ml milk
2 eggs
220g caster sugar
110g mashed banana
225g self-raising flour
75g frozen blueberries

1 Preheat oven to 200°C/180°C fan-assisted. Grease 12-hole (80ml) muffin pan.

2 Place butter and milk in small saucepan; stir over low heat until butter melts.

3 Beat eggs in small bowl with electric mixer until thick and creamy. Gradually add sugar, beating until dissolved between additions; stir in banana. Fold in sifted flour and cooled butter mixture, in two batches. Divide mixture among muffin pan holes.

4 Bake cakes 10 minutes. Remove pan from oven; press frozen blueberries into tops of cakes. Return to oven, bake further 15 minutes. Turn cakes onto wire racks to cool.

prep + cook time 50 minutes
makes 12
tip You will need one large (230g) over-ripe banana for this recipe.

WHITE CHOC-CHIP, ORANGE & CRANBERRY MINI CUPCAKES

300g self-raising flour
110g caster sugar
135g white chocolate chips
65g dried cranberries
60g butter, melted
180ml milk
1 egg
2 teaspoons finely grated orange
   rind
60ml) orange juice
cranberry icing
240g icing sugar
½ teaspoon vegetable oil
2 tablespoons cranberry juice,
   approximately

1 Preheat oven to 200°C/180°C fan-assisted. Line four 12-hole (20ml) mini muffin pans with paper cases.
2 Sift dry ingredients into medium bowl; stir in remaining ingredients.
3 Divide mixture among cases. Bake about 10 minutes. Stand muffins 2 minutes; turn, top-side up, onto wire rack to cool.
4 Meanwhile, make cranberry icing. Spread muffins with icing.
cranberry icing Sift icing sugar into small heatproof bowl. Stir in oil and enough juice to make a paste. Stir over small saucepan of simmering water until icing is spreadable.

prep + cook time 40 minutes
makes 48

CARAMEL CHOC-CHIP CAKES

90g white eating chocolate, chopped coarsely
90g unsalted butter, chopped coarsely
110g brown sugar
2 tablespoons golden syrup
125ml milk
110g plain flour
35g self-raising flour
1 egg
2 tablespoons milk chocolate chips
1 tablespoon icing sugar

1 Preheat oven to 160°C/140°C fan-assisted. Grease 9-hole large (125ml) muffin pan; line bases with baking parchment.
2 Stir chocolate, butter, brown sugar, syrup and milk in medium saucepan, over low heat, until smooth. Cool 15 minutes.
3 Whisk in sifted flours and egg. Stir in chocolate chips. Divide mixture among pan holes.
4 Bake cakes about 25 minutes. Stand cakes 5 minutes; turn, top-side up, onto wire rack to cool. Serve dusted with sifted icing sugar.

prep + cook time 45 minutes (+ standing)
makes 9

OTHER
SWEET TREATS

ROCK CAKES

300g self-raising flour
¼ teaspoon ground cinnamon
75g caster sugar
90g butter, chopped
160g sultanas
1 egg, beaten lightly
125ml milk
1 tablespoon caster sugar, extra

1 Preheat oven to 200°C/180°C fan-assisted. Grease oven trays.
2 Sift flour, cinnamon and sugar into medium bowl; rub in butter. Stir in sultanas, egg and milk. Do not over-mix.
3 Drop rounded tablespoons of mixture about 5cm apart onto trays; sprinkle with extra sugar.
4 Bake rock cakes about 15 minutes. Cool on trays.

prep + cook time 30 minutes
makes 18
nutritional count per rock cake
4.9g fat; 153 cal (640kJ)

SWIRLED CHOC-ALMOND BISCOTTI

60g butter
220g caster sugar
1 teaspoon vanilla essence
3 eggs
335g plain flour
1 teaspoon baking powder
½ teaspoon bicarbonate of soda
240g blanched almonds, chopped
   coarsely
25g cocoa powder
35g plain flour, extra

1 Beat butter, sugar and essence in medium bowl until just combined. Add eggs, one at a time, beating until combined between additions. Stir in flour, baking powder, soda and nuts. Cover, refrigerate 1 hour.
2 Preheat oven to 180°C/160°C fan-assisted.
3 Halve dough. Knead cocoa into one half of the dough; shape into a 30cm log. Knead extra flour into remaining dough; shape into a 30cm log.
4 Gently twist cocoa log and plain log together; place on lightly greased oven tray.
5 Bake about 45 minutes or until lightly browned and firm; stand 10 minutes.
6 Reduce oven temperature to 160°C/140°C fan-assisted.
7 Using serrated or electric knife, cut log, diagonally, into 1cm slices. Place slices on ungreased oven trays. Bake about 15 minutes or until dry and crisp, turning halfway through cooking; cool on wire racks.

prep + cook time 1 hour 30 minutes
makes 25

NUTTY MERINGUE STICKS

3 egg whites
165g caster sugar
120g ground hazelnuts
185g ground almonds
35g plain flour
100g dark eating chocolate,
  melted

1 Preheat oven to 160°C/140°C fan-assisted. Grease oven trays; line with baking parchment.
2 Beat egg whites in small bowl with electric mixer until foamy. Gradually beat in sugar, one tablespoon at a time, until dissolved between additions. Transfer mixture to large bowl.
3 Fold in ground nuts and sifted flour. Spoon mixture into large piping bag fitted with 1.5cm plain tube. Pipe 8cm sticks onto trays.
4 Bake about 15 minutes. Cool on trays 5 minutes; place on wire racks to cool.
5 Drizzle sticks with melted chocolate, place on baking-parchment-lined trays to set.

prep + cook time 45 minutes
makes 34

PINK MACAROONS

3 egg whites
2 tablespoons caster sugar
pink food colouring
200g icing sugar
120g ground almonds
2 tablespoons icing sugar, extra
white chocolate ganache
100g white eating chocolate,
   chopped coarsely
2 tablespoons whipping cream

1 Make white chocolate ganache.
2 Grease oven trays; line with baking parchment.
3 Beat egg whites in small bowl with electric mixer until soft peaks form. Add sugar and food colouring, beat until sugar dissolves. Transfer mixture to large bowl. Fold in sifted icing sugar and ground almonds, in two batches.
4 Spoon mixture into large piping bag fitted with 1.5cm plain tube. Pipe 36 x 4cm rounds, 2cm apart, onto trays. Tap trays on worktop to allow macaroons to spread slightly. Dust with sifted extra icing sugar; stand 15 minutes.
5 Preheat oven to 150°C/130°C fan-assisted.
6 Bake macaroons about 20 minutes. Stand 5 minutes; transfer to wire rack to cool.
7 Sandwich macaroons with ganache. Dust with a little sifted icing sugar, if desired.

white chocolate ganache Stir chocolate and cream in small saucepan over low heat until smooth. Transfer mixture to small bowl. Cover; refrigerate until mixture is spreadable.

prep + cook time 35 minutes (+ refrigeration + standing)
makes 18

RHUBARB & ALMOND CAKES

125ml milk
40g blanched almonds, toasted
80g butter, softened
1 teaspoon vanilla extract
110g caster sugar
2 eggs
150g self-raising flour
poached rhubarb
250g trimmed rhubarb, chopped
   coarsely
60ml water
110g granulated sugar

1 Preheat oven to 180°C/160°C fan-assisted. Grease a 6-hole large (180ml) muffin pan.
2 Make poached rhubarb.
3 Meanwhile, blend or process milk and nuts until smooth.
4 Beat butter, extract and sugar in small bowl with electric mixer until light and fluffy. Add eggs, one at a time, beating until just combined between additions (mixture might separate at this stage, but will come together later); transfer to large bowl. Stir in sifted flour and almond mixture.
5 Spoon mixture equally among muffin pan holes; bake 10 minutes. Carefully remove muffin pan from oven; divide drained rhubarb over muffins, bake further 15 minutes.
6 Stand muffins 5 minutes; turn, top-side up, onto wire rack to cool. Serve warm or cold with rhubarb syrup.

poached rhubarb Place ingredients in medium saucepan; bring to a boil. Reduce heat; simmer, uncovered, about 10 minutes or until rhubarb is just tender. Drain rhubarb over medium bowl; reserve rhubarb and syrup separately.

prep + cook time 1 hour
makes 6

MADELEINES

2 eggs
2 tablespoons caster sugar
2 tablespoons icing sugar
35g self-raising flour
35g plain flour
75g unsalted butter, melted
1 tablespoon water
2 tablespoons icing sugar, extra

1 Preheat oven to 200°C/180°C fan-assisted. Grease two 12-hole (30ml) madeleine pans.
2 Beat eggs and sifted sugars in small bowl with electric mixer until thick and creamy.
3 Meanwhile, triple-sift flours; sift flour over egg mixture. Pour combined butter and the water down side of bowl then fold ingredients together.
4 Drop rounded tablespoons of mixture into each pan hole. Bake about 10 minutes. Tap hot pan firmly on worktop to release madeleines then turn, top-side down, onto wire rack to cool. Serve dusted with sifted extra icing sugar.

prep + cook time 25 minutes
makes 24

ORANGE BLOSSOM & ALMOND CAKES

6 egg whites
185g unsalted butter, melted
2 tablespoons honey
1 tablespoon orange flower water
120g ground almonds
240g icing sugar
75g plain flour
40g flaked almonds
honey syrup
2 tablespoons honey
1 tablespoon water
2 teaspoons orange flower water

1 Preheat oven to 180°C/160°C fan-assisted. Grease individual fluted tart moulds (30ml) with butter. Place on oven tray.
2 Place egg whites in medium bowl; whisk lightly with fork until combined. Add butter, honey, orange flower water, ground almonds, sifted icing sugar and flour; stir until combined. Half fill the tart moulds with mixture; sprinkle with almonds.
3 Bake about 12 minutes. Stand cakes 5 minutes before turning top-side up onto wire rack to cool. Repeat with remaining mixture and almonds.
4 Meanwhile, make honey syrup.
5 Serve cakes drizzled with honey syrup.
honey syrup Combine honey and the water in small saucepan; bring to the boil. Remove from heat; stir in orange flower water. Allow to cool.

prep + cook time 40 minutes
makes 28

MINI CHOC-CHIP FRIANDS

4 egg whites
125g butter, melted
80g ground almonds
120g icing sugar
35g plain flour
100g dark eating chocolate,
    chopped finely
60ml pouring cream
100g dark eating chocolate,
    chopped, extra

1 Preheat oven to 200°C/180°C fan-assisted. Grease two 12-hole mini (40ml) muffin pans.
2 Place egg whites in medium bowl; beat with a fork. Stir in butter, ground almonds, sifted icing sugar and flour and chopped chocolate. Spoon mixture into pan holes.
3 Bake friands about 15 minutes. Stand friands in pans 5 minutes; turn, top-side up, onto wire rack to cool.
4 Meanwhile, combine cream and extra chocolate in small heatproof bowl over small saucepan of simmering water; stir until smooth. Stand until thickened. Spoon chocolate mixture over friands.

prep + cook time 40 minutes
makes 24

GINGERBREAD LOAVES

200g butter, softened
275g caster sugar
270g treacle
2 eggs
450g plain flour
1½ tablespoons ground ginger
3 teaspoons mixed spice
1 teaspoon bicarbonate of soda
180ml milk
vanilla icing
500g icing sugar
2 teaspoons butter, softened
½ teaspoon vanilla extract
80ml milk

1 Preheat oven to 200°C/180°C fan-assisted. Grease two eight-hole (125ml) mini loaf pans or line two muffin pans (80ml) with paper cases.
2 Beat butter and sugar in small bowl with electric mixer until light and fluffy. Pour in treacle, beat for 3 minutes. Add eggs one at a time, beating until just combined after each addition. Transfer mixture to large bowl. Stir in sifted dry ingredients, then milk. Divide mixture among prepared pans.
3 Bake loaves about 25 minutes. Stand 5 minutes before turning out onto wire rack to cool.
4 Spread icing over loaves; stand until set.

vanilla icing Sift icing sugar into heatproof bowl; stir in butter, vanilla and milk to form a smooth paste. Place bowl over simmering water; stir until icing is a spreadable consistency.

prep + cook time 1 hour
makes 16

MINI SULTANA LOAVES

125g butter, melted
375g sultanas
150g caster sugar
2 eggs
80ml buttermilk
75g plain flour
110g self-raising flour
lemon glacé icing
240g icing sugar
20g softened butter
2 tablespoons lemon juice,
   approximately

1 Preheat oven to 160°C/140°C fan-assisted. Grease 8-hole (180ml) mini loaf pan.
2 Stir ingredients in large bowl with wooden spoon until combined.
3 Divide mixture into pan holes, smooth tops; bake about 30 minutes. Stand cakes in pan 5 minutes before turning, top-side up, onto wire rack to cool.
4 Meanwhile, make lemon glacé icing. Drizzle icing over cakes.

lemon glacé icing Sift icing sugar into small heatproof bowl; stir in butter and enough juice to make a firm paste. Stir over small saucepan of simmering water until icing is pourable.

prep + cook time 55 minutes
makes 8

MIXED BERRY MUFFINS

335g self-raising flour
220g caster sugar
1 teaspoon vanilla extract
2 eggs, beaten lightly
100g butter, melted
250ml milk
1 teaspoon grated lemon rind
200g fresh or frozen mixed
  berries

1 Preheat oven to 200°C/180°C fan-assisted. Grease six-hole (180ml) muffin pan or spray six large disposable muffin cases with cooking oil spray and place on an oven tray.
2 Sift flour into large bowl; add sugar then combined extract, egg, butter, milk and rind. Add berries; stir through gently.
3 Divide muffin mixture among holes of prepared tray.
4 Bake muffins about 35 minutes. Stand muffins in tray for a few minutes before turning onto wire rack.

prep + cook time 45 minutes
makes 6

APPLE GINGER CAKES WITH LEMON ICING

250g butter, softened
330g dark brown sugar
3 eggs
90g golden syrup
300g plain flour
1½ teaspoons bicarbonate of
   soda
2 tablespoons ground ginger
1 tablespoon ground cinnamon
170g coarsely grated apple
160ml hot water
lemon icing
320g icing sugar
2 teaspoons butter, softened
80ml lemon juice

1 Preheat oven to 180°C/160°C fan-assisted. Grease two six-hole mini fluted tube pans or large muffin pans.

2 Beat butter and sugar in small bowl with electric mixer until light and fluffy. Add eggs, one at a time, beat until well combined between additions. Stir in syrup.

3 Transfer mixture to medium bowl; stir in sifted dry ingredients, then apple and the water.

4 Divide mixture among prepared pans, smooth tops.

5 Bake about 25 minutes. Stand cakes in pan 5 minutes then turn onto wire racks to cool.

6 Drizzle lemon icing over cakes.

lemon icing Sift icing sugar into medium heatproof bowl; stir in butter and juice to form a paste. Place bowl over small saucepan of simmering water; stir until icing is a pouring consistency.

prep + cook time 40 minutes
makes 12

GLOSSARY

almonds
blanched skins removed.
flaked paper-thin slices.
ground also known as almond meal; nuts are powdered to a coarse flour texture.
slivered cut lengthways.
baking powder a raising agent containing starch, but mostly cream of tartar and bicarbonate of soda in the proportions of 1 teaspoon cream of tartar to ½ teaspoon bicarbonate of soda. This is equal to 2 teaspoons baking powder.
bicarbonate of soda also known as baking soda; a mild alkali used as a leavening agent in baking.
buttermilk fresh low-fat milk cultured to give a slightly sour, tangy taste; low-fat yogurt or milk can be substituted.
cardamom can be bought in pod, seed or ground form. Has a distinctive, aromatic, sweetly rich flavour.
chocolate
chips hold their shape in baking.
dark eating made of cocoa liquor, cocoa butter and sugar.
milk eating most popular eating chocolate, mild and very sweet; similar in make-up to dark, but with the addition of milk solids.

white eating contains no cocoa solids, deriving its sweet flavour from cocoa butter. Is very sensitive to heat.
cinnamon dried inner bark of the shoots of the cinnamon tree. Available as a stick or ground.
cloves can be used whole or in ground form. Has a strong scent and taste so should be used minimally.
cocoa powder also known as unsweetened cocoa; cocoa beans that have been fermented, roasted, shelled, ground into powder then cleared of most of the fat content.
coconut
desiccated unsweetened and concentrated, dried finely shredded.
shredded thin strips of dried coconut. Available from health food stores and on line.
cornflour also known as cornstarch; used as a thickening agent in cooking.
cranberries, dried have the same slightly sour, succulent flavour as fresh cranberries. Can usually be substituted for or with other dried fruit in most recipes. Available in most supermarkets. Also available in sweetened form.

cream we used fresh cream in this book, unless otherwise stated. Also known as pure cream and pouring cream; has no additives unlike commercially thickened cream. Minimum fat content 35%.
soured a thick commercially-cultured soured cream. Minimum fat content 35%.
whipping a cream that contains a thickener. Has a minimum fat content of 35 per cent.
cream cheese a soft cow's milk cheese with a fat content ranging from 14 per cent to 33 per cent.
custard powder instant mixture used to make pouring custard; similar to North American instant pudding mixes.
essences synthetically produced substances used in small amounts to impart their respective flavours to foods. An extract is made by actually extracting the flavour from a food product. In the case of vanilla, pods are soaked, usually in alcohol, to capture the authentic flavour. Both extracts and essences will keep indefinitely if stored in a cool dark place.
flour
plain all-purpose flour.
rice extremely fine flour made from ground rice.

self-raising plain flour sifted with baking powder (a raising agent consisting mainly of 2 parts cream of tartar to 1 part bicarbonate of soda) in the proportion of 150g flour to 2 level teaspoons baking powder.

wholemeal also known as wholewheat flour; milled with the wheat germ so is higher in fibre and more nutritional than plain flour.

food colouring vegetable-based substance available in liquid, paste or gel form.

gelatine we used powdered gelatine; also available in sheet form known as leaf gelatine.

ginger

ground the dried ground root of a tropical plant.

stem fresh ginger root preserved in sugar syrup.

glucose syrup also known as liquid glucose.

ground hazelnuts made by grinding hazelnuts to a coarse flour texture for use in baking or as a thickening agent.

golden syrup a by-product of refined sugarcane; pure maple syrup or honey can be substituted if preferred.

maple syrup distilled from the sap of maple trees found only in Canada and parts of North America. Maple-flavoured syrup is not an adequate substitute for the real thing.

mixed peel candied citrus peel.

mixed spice a blend of ground spices usually consisting of cinnamon, allspice and nutmeg.

marzipan a paste made from ground almonds, sugar and water. Similar to almond paste but sweeter, more pliable and finer in texture. Easily coloured and rolled to cover cakes or make into shapes.

orange flower water concentrated flavouring made from orange blossoms.

passionfruit a small tropical fruit, native to Brazil, comprised of a tough dark-purple skin surrounding edible black sweet-sour seeds.

peanuts also known as groundnut, not in fact a nut but the pod of a legume. We mainly use raw (unroasted) or unsalted roasted peanuts.

peanut butter a paste made from ground roasted peanuts.

rolled oats traditional whole oat grains that have been steamed and flattened. Not the quick-cook variety.

sugar we used coarse, granulated table sugar, also known as crystal sugar, unless otherwise specified.

caster also known as superfine or finely granulated table sugar.

dark brown an extremely soft, fine-grained sugar retaining the deep flavour and colour of molasses.

icing also known as confectioner's sugar or powdered sugar.

light brown another soft, fine-grained sugar with cane molasses added.

treacle thick, dark syrup not unlike molasses; a by-product of sugar refining.

vanilla extract obtained from vanilla beans infused in water; a non-alcoholic version of essence.

walnuts large nut with distinctive ridged kernels. Walnuts contain the beneficial omega-3 fatty acids, which is terrific news for people who dislike the taste of fish.

wheat germ the inner embryo of the wheat kernel. It is rich in vitamins and minerals and is discarded when wheat is milled into white flour. Store in the refrigerator.

INDEX

CONVERSION CHARTS

measures

One metric tablespoon holds 20ml; one metric teaspoon holds 5ml.

All cup and spoon measurements are level. The most accurate way of measuring dry ingredients is to weigh them. When measuring liquids, use a clear glass or plastic jug with metric markings.

We use large eggs with an average weight of 60g.

dry measures

METRIC	IMPERIAL
15g	½oz
30g	1oz
60g	2oz
90g	3oz
125g	4oz (¼lb)
155g	5oz
185g	6oz
220g	7oz
250g	8oz (½lb)
280g	9oz
315g	10oz
345g	11oz
375g	12oz (¾lb)
410g	13oz
440g	14oz
470g	15oz
500g	16oz (1lb)
750g	24oz (1½lb)
1kg	32oz (2lb)

liquid measures

METRIC	IMPERIAL
30ml	1 fluid oz
60ml	2 fluid oz
100ml	3 fluid oz
125ml	4 fluid oz
150ml	5 fluid oz
190ml	6 fluid oz
250ml	8 fluid oz
300ml	10 fluid oz
500ml	16 fluid oz
600ml	20 fluid oz
1000ml (1 litre)	32 fluid oz

length measures

3mm	⅛in
6mm	¼in
1cm	½in
2cm	¾in
2.5cm	1in
5cm	2in
6cm	2½in
8cm	3in
10cm	4in
13cm	5in
15cm	6in
18cm	7in
20cm	8in
23cm	9in
25cm	10in
28cm	11in
30cm	12in (1ft)

oven temperatures

These are fan-assisted temperatures. If you have a conventional oven (ie. not fan-assisted), increase temperatures by 10–20°.

	°C (CELSIUS)	°F (FAHRENHEIT)	GAS MARK
Very low	100	210	½
Low	130	260	1–2
Moderately low	140	280	3
Moderate	160	325	4–5
Moderately hot	180	350	6
Hot	200	400	7–8
Very hot	220	425	9